My
Smile

This diary belongs to:

_____

☆ THINGS I AM NERVOUS ABOUT ☆

☆ MY DREAM BEDROOM ☆

☆ MY DREAM CAREER ☆

MY FAVORITE TIME OF DAY

☆ IF I COULD MEET ANYONE, ☆
IT WOULD BE . . .

☆ MY LEAST FAVORITE FOOD ☆

☆ WAYS I CAN HELP MY COMMUNITY ☆

☆ SOMETHING KIND I DID RECENTLY ☆

☆ I'M NOT PERFECT, BUT I TRY MY BEST ☆

HOW I SEE MYSELF
VS. HOW OTHERS SEE ME

☆ WHAT NO ONE KNOWS ABOUT ME ☆

☆ I WISH I HAD MORE TIME TO . . . ☆

☆ IF I HAD A TIME MACHINE, I WOULD . . . ☆

☆ MY EARLIEST MEMORY ☆

☆ A DREAM I HAD ☆

☆ A FRIEND I TALKED TO ☆

☆ THINGS I AM EXCITED ABOUT ☆

☆ BOOKS I READ THAT I LOVED ☆

WOW. THAT IS ONE HUGE BOOK!

IT'S MY FAVORITE BOOK IN THE WORLD.

PUBLISHED IN 1932 AND REPRINTED THIRTY-FOUR TIMES, IT INCLUDES PHOTOGRAPHS OF BROADWAY SET AND STAGE DESIGN FROM THE NINETEEN-TEENS AND TWENTIES...

☆ A PLACE I LIKE TO GO TO THINK ☆

☆ A FUNNY JOKE I HEARD ☆

All rights reserved.
Published in the United States by Clarkson Potter/
Publishers, an imprint of Random House, a division
of Penguin Random House LLC, New York.

clarksonpotter.com

CLARKSON POTTER is a trademark and POTTER
with colophon is a registered trademark of
Penguin Random House LLC.

ISBN 978-0-593-13562-4

Printed in China

Diary design by Nicole Block
Cover design by Danielle Deschenes and Nicole Block

10 9 8 7 6 5 4 3 2 1